SERVES 8–10

PREPARATION 30 min

COOKING 1 h

DIFFICULTY level 1

Zucchini Cake

Preheat the oven to 350°F (180°C/gas 4). • Butter an 11 x 7-inch (28 x 18-cm) baking pan. • Mix the flour, cinnamon, baking powder, baking soda, and salt in a large bowl. • Beat the sugar, butter, and vanilla in a large bowl with an electric mixer at medium speed until pale and creamy. • Add the eggs, one at a time, beating until just blended after each addition. • With mixer at low speed, gradually beat in the dry ingredients. • By hand, stir in the zucchini and walnuts. • Spoon the batter into the prepared pan. • Bake for about 1 hour, or until a toothpick inserted into the center comes out clean. • Cool the cake in the pan for 15 minutes. Turn out onto a rack to cool completely. • Vanilla Frosting: Mix the confectioners' sugar, butter, and vanilla extract in a medium bowl. Beat in enough of the water to make a spreadable frosting. Spread the top of the cake with the frosting.

2 cups (300 g) all-purpose (plain) flour
2 teaspoons cinnamon
1 teaspoon baking powder
1/2 teaspoon baking soda (bicarbonate of soda)
1/4 teaspoon salt
2 cups (400 g) sugar
1 cup (250 ml) butter
1 teaspoon vanilla extract (essence)
3 large eggs
2 cups (300 g) grated zucchini
1 cup (150 g) coarsely chopped walnuts

Vanilla Frosting
2 cups (300 g) confectioners' (icing) sugar
2 tablespoons butter, melted
1 teaspoon vanilla extract (essence)
3 tablespoons boiling water

TREATS

just great recipes

GENERAL INFORMATION

The level of difficulty of the recipes in this book
is expressed as a number from 1 (simple) to 3 (difficult).

TREATS
just great recipes
cakes

M^CRAE BOOKS

SERVES 10–12

PREPARATION 30 min

COOKING 45–55 min

DIFFICULTY level 2

Lime Cake
with honey syrup

Cake: Preheat the oven to 350°F (180°C/gas 4). • Butter and flour a 9-inch (23-cm) Bundt pan. • Stir the flour, coconut, almonds, baking powder, and salt in a large bowl. • Beat the butter, sugar, and lime zest in a large bowl with an electric mixer at medium speed until creamy. • Add the eggs, one at a time, beating until just blended after each addition. • With mixer at low speed, gradually beat in the dry ingredients, alternating with the yogurt and lime juice. • Spoon the batter into the prepared pan. • Bake for 45–55 minutes, or until a toothpick inserted into the center comes out clean. • Cool in the pan for 10 minutes. Turn out onto a rack. Place the cake on the rack in a jelly-roll pan. • Lime and Honey Syrup: Peel the limes and slice the zest into thin strips. Squeeze the juice from the limes and place in a small saucepan with the zest, water, honey, and cardamom pods. Bring to a boil over low heat and simmer for 5 minutes. Strain to remove the cardamom. Poke holes in the cake with a skewer. • Pour the syrup over the hot cake.

Cake

2½ cups (375 g) all-purpose (flour) flour

¾ cup (120 g) shredded (desiccated) coconut

¼ cup (30 g) finely ground almonds

2 teaspoons baking powder

¼ teaspoon salt

1 cup (250 g) butter, softened

1 cup (200 g) sugar

1 tablespoon finely grated lime zest

3 large eggs

¾ cup (180 ml) plain yogurt

2 tablespoons freshly squeezed lime juice

Lime and Honey Syrup

2 limes

½ cup (125 ml) cold water

¼ cup (60 ml) honey

4 cardamom pods, smashed with flat side of chef's knife

SERVES 8–10

PREPARATION 25 min

COOKING 30–40 min

DIFFICULTY level I

Lemon Crown
with glaze

Preheat the oven to 400°F (200°C/gas 6). • Butter and flour a 9-inch (23-cm) tube pan. • Mix the flour, baking powder, and salt in a medium bowl. • Beat the butter, sugar, and lemon zest in a large bowl with an electric mixer at medium speed until creamy. • Add the eggs, one at a time, beating until just blended after each addition. • With mixer at low speed, gradually beat in the dry ingredients and 2 tablespoons of lemon juice. • Spoon the batter into the prepared pan. • Bake for 30–40 minutes, or until a toothpick inserted into the center comes out clean. • Cool the cake in the pan for 15 minutes. Turn out onto a rack to cool completely. • Warm the apricot preserves in a saucepan and spread over the cake. • Beat the confectioners' sugar and enough of the remaining lemon juice to make a thin glaze. Drizzle over the cake. • Decorate with the candied peel, if desired.

1²/₃ cups (250 g) all-purpose (plain) flour
2 teaspoons baking powder
¼ teaspoon salt
³/₄ cup (180 g) butter, softened
1¼ cups (250 g) sugar
2 tablespoons finely grated lemon zest
3 large eggs
⅓ cup (90 ml) freshly squeezed lemon juice
½ cup (150 g) apricot preserves (jam)
1²/₃ cups (250 g) confectioners' (icing) sugar
Candied orange, lemon, and lime peel, cut into strips, to decorate (optional)

Lemon Crown
with frosting

Preheat the oven to 350°F (180°C/gas 4). • Butter and flour a 9-inch (23-cm) tube pan. • Mix the flour, baking powder, and salt in a medium bowl. • Beat the butter, sugar, lemon zest, and both extracts in a large bowl with an electric mixer at medium speed until creamy. • Add the eggs, one at a time, beating until just blended after each addition. • With mixer at low speed, gradually beat in the dry ingredients, alternating with the milk. • Spoon the batter into the prepared pan. • Bake for 40–50 minutes, or until a toothpick inserted into the center comes out clean. • Cool the cake in the pan for 10 minutes. Turn out onto a rack to cool. • Frosting: Mix the confectioners' sugar, butter, and lemon extract in a medium bowl. Beat in enough of the lemon juice to make a spreadable frosting. Spread the top of the cake with the frosting.

Cake

2 cups (300 g) all-purpose (plain) flour

2 teaspoons baking powder

1/4 teaspoon salt

1/2 cup (125 g) butter, softened

1 cup (200 g) sugar

1 tablespoon finely grated lemon zest

1 teaspoon lemon extract (essence)

1/2 teaspoon vanilla (essence) extract

3 large eggs

2 tablespoons milk

Frosting

1 1/2 cups (225 g) confectioners' (icing) sugar

2 tablespoons butter, melted

1 teaspoon lemon extract (essence)

1–2 tablespoons freshly squeezed lemon juice

SERVES 8–10

PREPARATION 30 min

COOKING 1 h

DIFFICULTY level 1

Coffee Ring
with frosting

Preheat the oven to 350°F (180°C/gas 4). • Butter and flour a 9-inch (23-cm) tube pan. • Mix the flour, baking powder, baking soda, and salt in a large bowl. • Beat the butter, sugar, and vanilla in a large bowl with an electric mixer at medium speed until pale and creamy. • Add the eggs, one at a time, beating until just blended after each addition. • With mixer at low speed, gradually beat in the dry ingredients, alternating with the sour cream. • Transfer one-third of the batter to a small bowl and stir in the coffee. • Spoon half the plain batter into the prepared pan. Spoon the coffee-flavored batter over the top. Spread the remaining batter on top. • Bake for about 1 hour, or until golden brown and a toothpick inserted into the center comes out clean. • Cool the cake in the pan for 15 minutes. Turn out onto a rack to cool. • Frosting: Stir the coffee mixture into the confectioners' sugar in a small bowl. • Spread over the cake.

2 cups (300 g) all-purpose (plain) flour
1 teaspoon baking powder
1/2 teaspoon baking soda (bicarbonate of soda)
1/4 teaspoon salt
1 cup (250 g) butter
1 cup (200 g) sugar
2 teaspoons vanilla extract (essence)
2 large eggs
1 cup (250 ml) sour cream
2 tablespoons freeze-dried coffee granules dissolved in 1 tablespoon boiling water

Frosting
2 teaspoons freeze-dried coffee granules dissolved in 2–3 tablespoons hot strong coffee
2 cups (300 g) confectioners' (icing) sugar

Poppy Seed Cake

Cake: Bring the milk to a boil in a small saucepan over medium-low heat. Remove from the heat. Stir in the poppy seeds and set aside to cool. • Preheat the oven to 350°F (180°C/gas 4). • Butter and flour two 8-inch (20-cm) round cake pans. • Mix the flour, baking powder, and salt in a medium bowl. • Beat the butter, 1 cup (200 g) of sugar, and vanilla in a large bowl with an electric mixer at medium speed until creamy. • With mixer at low speed, gradually beat in the dry ingredients, alternating with the milk and poppy seeds. • With mixer at medium speed, beat the egg whites in a large bowl until frothy. With mixer at high speed, gradually add the remaining sugar, beating until stiff, glossy peaks form. • Use a large rubber spatula to fold the beaten whites into the batter. • Spoon half the batter into each of the prepared pans. • Bake for 30–40 minutes, or until a toothpick inserted into the center comes out clean. • Cool the cakes in the pans for 10 minutes. Turn out onto racks and let cool completely. • Cream Cheese Frosting: With mixer at medium speed, beat the cream cheese, butter, confectioners' sugar, and vanilla until smooth. • Place one cake on a serving plate. Spread with one-third of the frosting. Top with the remaining cake and spread the top and sides with the remaining frosting. • To decorate: Cut 4 strips of cardboard and lay them diagonally across the cake. Sprinkle with the poppy seeds, then carefully remove the cardboard.

Cake
1 cup (250 ml) milk
$1/2$ cup (75 g) poppy seeds
2 cups (300 g) all-purpose (plain) flour
$2 1/2$ teaspoons baking powder
$1/4$ teaspoon salt
$3/4$ cup (180 g) butter, softened
$1 1/4$ cups (250 g) sugar
2 teaspoons vanilla extract (essence)
3 large egg whites

Cream Cheese Frosting
1 package (8 oz/250 g) cream cheese, softened
$1/4$ cup (60 g) butter, softened
$2 1/2$ cups (375 g) confectioners' (icing) sugar
2 teaspoons vanilla extract (essence)
3 tablespoons poppy seeds, to decorate

SERVES 8–10

PREPARATION 40 min

COOKING 50–60 min

DIFFICULTY level 2

Butter Cake
with hazelnut frosting

Preheat the oven to 350°F (180°C/gas 4). • Butter and flour a 10-inch (25-cm) springform pan. • Stir the flour, cornstarch, baking powder, and salt in a large bowl. • Beat the butter, sugar, orange and lemon zests, and vanilla in a large bowl with an electric mixer at medium speed until creamy. • Add the eggs, one at a time, beating until just blended after each addition. • With mixer at low speed, gradually add the dry ingredients, alternating with the milk. • Spoon the batter into the prepared pan. • Bake for 50–60 minutes, or until a toothpick inserted into the center comes out clean. • Cool the cake in the pan on a rack for 15 minutes. Loosen and remove the pan sides. Invert the cake onto the rack. Remove the pan bottom and let cool completely. • Hazelnut Frosting: Beat the cream cheese, sugar, hazelnut oil, rum, and vanilla until smooth. • With mixer at high speed, beat the cream in a medium bowl until thick. Fold into the cream cheese mixture. • Split the cake horizontally. Place one layer on a serving plate and spread with one-third of the frosting. Top with the remaining layer. Spread the top and sides with one-third of the frosting. Spoon the remaining frosting into a pastry bag. Pipe a crisscross pattern over the cake. Decorate with the hazelnuts.

2¹⁄₃ cups (350 g) all-purpose (plain) flour
1 cup (150 g) cornstarch (cornflour)
2 teaspoons baking powder
¹⁄₄ teaspoon salt
1 cup (250 g) butter, softened
1 cup (200 g) sugar
1 tablespoon finely grated orange zest
1 tablespoon finely grated lemon zest
1 teaspoon vanilla extract (essence)
5 large eggs
¹⁄₂ cup (125 ml) milk

Hazelnut Frosting
1 package (8 oz/250 g) cream cheese, softened
¹⁄₂ cup (100 g) sugar
2 teaspoons hazelnut oil
1¹⁄₂ teaspoons rum
1 teaspoon vanilla extract (essence)
1 cup (250 ml) heavy (double) cream
10 whole hazelnuts, to decorate

Butter Cake
with walnut crunch

SERVES 8–10

PREPARATION 20 min

COOKING 50–60 min

DIFFICULTY level 1

Preheat the oven to 350°F (180°C/gas 4). • Butter and flour a 9-inch (23-cm) tube pan. • Crunch: Combine the brown sugar, flour, and cinnamon in a medium bowl. Use a pastry blender to cut in the butter until the mixture resembles fine crumbs. Stir in half the walnuts. • Cake: Stir the flour, baking powder, nutmeg, and salt in a medium bowl. • Beat the butter, brown sugar, and vanilla in a large bowl with an electric mixer at medium speed until creamy. • Add the eggs, one at a time, beating until just blended after each addition. • With mixer at low speed, gradually add the dry ingredients, alternating with the orange juice. • Spoon the walnut crunch into the prepared pan. Cover with the batter. Top with the remaining walnuts. • Bake for 50–60 minutes, or until golden brown. • Cool the cake in the pan on a rack. Turn out, turn walnut-side up, and serve warm.

Walnut Crunch
¾ cup (150 g) firmly packed brown sugar
⅓ cup (50 g) all-purpose (plain) flour
½ teaspoon cinnamon
¼ cup (60 g) cold butter, cut up
¾ cup (90 g) walnuts, coarsely chopped

Cake
2 cups (300 g) all-purpose (plain) flour
2 teaspoons baking powder
½ teaspoon nutmeg
¼ teaspoon salt
½ cup (125 g) butter, softened
¾ cup (150 g) firmly packed brown sugar
1 teaspoon vanilla extract (essence)
4 large eggs
¾ cup (180 ml) freshly squeezed orange juice

SERVES 8–10

PREPARATION 15 min

COOKING 55 min

DIFFICULTY level 1

Brunch Cake

Preheat the oven to 350°F (180°C/gas 4). • Butter a 9-inch (23-cm) square baking pan. • Beat the brown sugar, flour, eggs, butter, vanilla, cinnamon, nutmeg, baking powder, baking soda, and salt in a large bowl with an electric mixer at medium speed until well blended, about 3 minutes. • Stir in the apples, nuts, and raisins. • Spoon the batter into the prepared pan. • Bake for about 55 minutes, or until a toothpick inserted into the center comes out clean. • Cool the cake in the pan on a rack for 10 minutes. Serve warm.

1¼ cups (250 g) firmly packed brown sugar

1½ cups (225 g) all-purpose (plain) flour

3 large eggs

¼ cup (60 g) butter

1 teaspoon vanilla extract (essence)

1 teaspoon each ground cinnamon and nutmeg

1 teaspoon baking powder

½ teaspoon baking soda (bicarbonate of soda)

¼ teaspoon salt

2 medium tart apples, grated

1½ cups (180 g) walnuts, coarsely chopped

1 cup (180 g) raisins

Viennois

Preheat the oven to 300°F (150°C/gas 2). • Butter two 8-inch (20-cm) round cake pans. Line with parchment paper. Butter the paper. • Mix the cocoa, flour, cornstarch, and salt in a medium bowl. • Beat the sugar and egg yolks in a large bowl with an electric mixer at high speed until pale and thick. • With mixer at low speed, gradually beat in the dry ingredients • With mixer at high speed, beat the egg whites in a large bowl until stiff peaks form. Fold them into the batter. • Spoon half the batter into each of the prepared pans. • Bake for 20–25 minutes, or until springy to the touch and a toothpick inserted into the center comes out clean. • Cool the cakes in the pans for 10 minutes. Turn out onto racks. Carefully remove the paper and let cool completely. • Split the cakes horizontally. Place one layer on a serving plate and spread with some frosting. Repeat with 2 more layers. Top with the remaining layer. Spread the top and sides with the remaining frosting. • Sprinkle the chocolate over the top of the cake.

$\frac{1}{4}$ cup (30 g) unsweetened cocoa powder

$2\frac{1}{2}$ tablespoons cake flour

$2\frac{1}{2}$ tablespoons cornstarch (cornflour)

$\frac{1}{4}$ teaspoon salt

$1\frac{1}{2}$ cups (300 g) semifine (caster) sugar

8 large eggs, separated

2 cups (500 g) Chocolate Rum Frosting (see page 22)

2 oz (60 g) dark chocolate, finely grated

SERVES 8–10

PREPARATION 45 min

COOKING 40 min

DIFFICULTY level 2

Chocolate Cake
with hazelnut cream

Butter and flour two 8-inch (20-cm) springform pans. • Melt the chocolate in a double boiler over barely simmering water. Set aside to cool. • Mix the flour, baking powder, and salt in a medium bowl. • Beat the egg yolks, sugar, and almond extract in a medium bowl with an electric mixer at high speed until pale and thick. • With mixer at low speed, gradually beat in the dry ingredients, alternating with the chocolate and cream. • Beat the egg whites until stiff and fold into the batter. • Spoon half the batter into each of the prepared pans. • Turn the oven on to 400°F (200°C/gas 6) and put the cakes in while it is still cold. Bake for 25 minutes. Turn the oven down to 300°F (150°C/gas 2) and bake for 15 more minutes. • Cool the cakes in the pans for 10 minutes. Loosen and remove the pan sides. Invert onto racks to cool completely. • Hazelnut Cream: Bring the cream to a boil in a saucepan. Remove from the heat. Stir in the chocolate hazelnut cream and butter until smooth. • Refrigerate for 30 minutes. • Split the cakes horizontally. • Place one layer on a serving plate and spread with filling. Repeat with 2 more layers. Top with the remaining layer. Spread the top and sides with the remaining filling. • Dust with the cocoa and top with the raspberries.

4 oz (125 g) dark chocolate, coarsely chopped
1⅓ cups all-purpose (plain) flour
1½ teaspoons baking powder
¼ teaspoon salt
3 large eggs, separated
⅓ cup (75 g) sugar
½ teaspoon almond extract (essence)
½ cup (125 ml) heavy (double) cream

Hazelnut Cream
1 cup (250 ml) heavy (double) cream
1½ cups chocolate hazelnut cream (Nutella)
⅓ cup (90 g) butter, cut up
¼ cup (30 g) unsweetened cocoa powder, to dust
Fresh raspberries, to decorate

Chocolate Cake

with marble swirl frosting

Preheat the oven to 350°F (180°C/gas 4). • Butter a 9-inch (23-cm) square baking pan. Line with parchment paper. Butter the paper. • Beat the flour, sugar, cocoa, baking powder, salt, butter, eggs, milk, water, vanilla, and vinegar in a large bowl with an electric mixer at medium speed until creamy. • Spoon the batter into the prepared pan. • Bake for 50–60 minutes, or until the cake shrinks from the pan sides and a toothpick inserted into the center comes out clean. • Cool the cake in the pan for 5 minutes. Turn out onto a rack. Carefully remove the paper and let cool completely. • Chocolate Frosting: Melt the chocolate and butter in a double boiler over barely simmering water. Set aside to cool enough to spread (make sure it doesn't set). • Cream Cheese Frosting: With mixer at medium speed, beat the cream cheese and butter in a small bowl until creamy. Add the honey and gradually beat in the confectioners' sugar. • Spread the cake with the cream cheese frosting. Place spoonfuls of chocolate frosting over the top. Use a fork to swirl the frostings together to create a marbled effect.

2⅓ cups (350 g) all-purpose (plain) flour
1½ cups (300 g) sugar
⅔ cup (100 g) unsweetened cocoa powder
2½ teaspoons baking powder
¼ teaspoon salt
¾ cup (180 g) butter, softened
3 large eggs
1 cup (250 ml) milk
½ cup (125 ml) boiling water
1 teaspoon vanilla extract (essence)
1 teaspoon white wine vinegar

Chocolate Frosting
4 oz (125 g) dark chocolate, coarsely chopped
½ cup (125 g) butter

Cream Cheese Frosting
1 package (8 oz/250 g) cream cheese, softened
⅓ cup (90 g) butter, softened
1 tablespoon honey
1½ cups (225 g) confectioners' (icing) sugar

SERVES 10–12

PREPARATION 30 min

COOKING 50 min

DIFFICULTY level 1

Chocolate Cake
with sour cream

Preheat the oven to 350°F (180°C/gas 4). • Butter and flour two 9-inch (23-cm) cake pans. • Stir the water, cocoa, and baking soda in a saucepan over low heat until smooth. Set aside to cool. • Mix the flour, cornstarch, and salt in a medium bowl. • Beat the butter, sugar, and vanilla in a large bowl with an electric mixer at medium speed until creamy. • Add the eggs, one at a time, beating until just blended after each addition. • With mixer at low speed, gradually beat in the dry ingredients, alternating with the sour cream and cocoa mixture. • Spoon half the batter into each of the prepared pans. • Bake for about 50 minutes, or until a toothpick inserted into the center comes out clean. • Cool the cakes in the pans for 5 minutes. Turn out onto racks to cool completely. • Chocolate Rum Frosting: Mix the confectioners' sugar and cocoa in a large bowl. Add the butter, rum, and vanilla. Beat in enough of the milk to make a thick, spreadable frosting. • Place a cake on a serving plate. Spread with one-third of the frosting. Top with the remaining cake. Spread the top and sides with the remaining frosting.

$1/2$ cup (125 ml) water
$1/2$ cup (75 g) unsweetened cocoa powder
2 teaspoons baking soda (bicarbonate of soda)
2 cups (300 g) all-purpose (plain) flour
$1/2$ cup (75 g) cornstarch (cornflour)
$1/4$ teaspoon salt
$2/3$ cup (150 g) butter
$1 3/4$ cups (350 g) sugar
$1 1/2$ teaspoons vanilla extract (essence)
2 large eggs
1 cup (250 ml) sour cream

Chocolate Rum Frosting
3 cups (450 g) confectioners' (icing) sugar
$1/2$ cup (75 g) unsweetened cocoa powder
$3/4$ cup (180 g) butter, softened
2 tablespoons rum
1 teaspoon vanilla extract (essence)
1–2 tablespoons milk

SERVES 10–12

PREPARATION 40 min

COOKING 35 min

DIFFICULTY level 2

Chocolate Cake
with peppermint cream

Preheat the oven to 350°F (180°C/gas 4). • Butter a 9-inch (23-cm) round cake pan. Line with parchment paper. Butter the paper. • Melt the chocolate and water in a double boiler over barely simmering water. Set aside to cool. • Mix the flour, cocoa, baking powder, baking soda, and salt in a medium bowl. • Beat the butter and both sugars in a large bowl with an electric mixer at medium speed until creamy. • Add the eggs, one at a time, beating until just blended after each addition. • With mixer at low speed, gradually beat in the dry ingredients, alternating with the milk and chocolate. • Spoon the batter into the prepared pan. • Bake for about 35 minutes, or until a toothpick inserted into the center comes out clean. • Cool the cake in the pan for 10 minutes. Turn out onto a rack. Carefully remove the paper and let cool completely. • Peppermint Filling: With mixer at high speed, beat the confectioners' sugar and butter in a medium bowl until creamy. Stir in the milk and peppermint extract. • Chocolate Frosting: Stir together the confectioners' sugar and cocoa in a medium bowl. Beat in the butter and enough water to make a thick, spreadable frosting. • Split the cake horizontally. • Place one layer on a serving plate. Spread with the filling. Top with the remaining layer. Spread the top and sides with the frosting.

4 oz (125 g) dark chocolate, coarsely chopped

1/4 cup (60 ml) water

1 1/3 cups (200 g) all-purpose (plain) flour

2 tablespoons unsweetened cocoa powder

1 teaspoon baking powder

1 teaspoon baking soda (bicarbonate of soda)

1/4 teaspoon salt

1/2 cup (125 g) butter, melted

1 cup (200 g) sugar

1/3 cup (70 g) firmly packed brown sugar

2 large eggs

1/3 cup (90 ml) milk

Peppermint Filling

2 cups (300 g) confectioners' (icing) sugar

1/4 cup (60 g) butter

1 tablespoon milk

1 teaspoon peppermint extract (essence)

Chocolate Frosting

3 cups (450 g) confectioners' (icing) sugar

4 tablespoons unsweetened cocoa powder

3 tablespoons butter

2–3 tablespoons boiling water

Babà Cake

Cake: Preheat the oven to 350°F (180°C/gas 4). • Butter a 9 x 5-inch (23 x 12-cm) loaf pan. Line with parchment paper. • Mix the flour, baking powder, and salt in a medium bowl. • Beat the sugar and egg yolks in a large bowl with an electric mixer at high speed until pale and thick. • With mixer at low speed, gradually beat in the dry ingredients. • With mixer at high speed, beat the egg whites in a large bowl until stiff peaks form. Use a large rubber spatula to fold them into the batter. • Spoon the batter into the prepared pan. • Bake for 30–40 minutes, or until springy to the touch and a toothpick inserted into the center comes out clean. • Cool the cake in the pan for 10 minutes. Turn out onto a rack. Carefully remove the paper and let cool completely. • Orange Syrup: Mix the orange juice and Marsala in a small bowl. Place the cake on a serving plate. Poke holes all over the cake and drizzle with the syrup. Serve the remaining syrup on the side.

Cake
1 cup (150 g) all-purpose (plain) flour
2 teaspoons baking powder
1/4 teaspoon salt
1 1/4 cups (250 g) sugar
4 large eggs, separated

Orange Syrup
1 cup (250 ml) freshly squeezed orange juice
1/3 cup (90 ml) dry Marsala wine or sherry

SERVES 8–10
PREPARATION 1 h + 3 h to chill + time
to prepare sponge
COOKING 35–40 min
DIFFICULTY level 3

Orange Gâteau

Prepare the sponge. • Filling: Beat the egg yolks, orange zest, and sugar in a saucepan until well blended. Stir over low heat until the mixture lightly coats a metal spoon. Place the pan in a bowl of ice water and stir until cooled. • Sprinkle the gelatin over the orange and lemon juices in a saucepan. Stir over low heat until the gelatin has dissolved. Remove from the heat. • Fold the egg mixture into the gelatin mixture. • Beat the cream in a large bowl until stiff. Fold into the egg mixture. • Split the sponge horizontally. Drizzle with the orange liqueur. • Place a sponge layer on a plate and surround with 9-inch (23-cm) springform pan sides. Spread with the filling. Top with the remaining sponge layer. • Refrigerate for 3 hours. • Remove the pan sides. • Warm the apricot preserves over low heat. Brush over the cake. Stick the almonds onto the sides. • Melt the butter and sugar in a saucepan over low heat. Add the orange slices and simmer until the oranges begin to caramelize, about 10 minutes. Arrange the oranges around the edge of the cake. Decorate with star fruit and candied cherries.

1 Basic Sponge Cake (see page 30)

Filling
4 large egg yolks
Finely grated zest of 1 orange
1/2 cup (100 g) sugar
2 tablespoons unflavored gelatin
Freshly squeezed juice of 3 oranges
1 tablespoon freshly squeezed lemon juice
3/4 cup (180 ml) heavy (double) cream
2 tablespoons orange liqueur

Topping
1/2 cup (150 g) apricot preserves (jam)
3/4 cup (100 g) flaked almonds
1/4 cup (60 g) butter
1/2 cup (100 g) sugar
2 oranges, thinly sliced
Sliced star fruit and candied cherries, to decorate

SERVES 8–10

PREPARATION 45 min + 2 h to chill +
time to prepare sponge

DIFFICULTY level 2

Raspberry Gateau

Prepare the sponge. • Place the raspberries, 1 cup (150 g) of confectioners' sugar, and kirsch in a large bowl. Soak 1 hour. • Drain the raspberries, reserving the syrup. • Beat the cream cheese, remaining confectioners' sugar, and lemon zest in a large bowl with an electric mixer at medium speed until creamy. With mixer at low speed, beat in the raspberries. • Sprinkle the gelatin over the water in a saucepan. Let stand 1 minute. Stir over low heat until the gelatin has dissolved. • With mixer at high speed, beat the cream in a medium bowl until stiff. Use a large rubber spatula to fold the cream and the gelatin mixture into the raspberry mixture. • Split the sponge in three horizontally. Place one layer on a serving plate. Brush with the syrup. Spread with half the raspberry mixture. Top with a second layer and spread with the remaining raspberry mixture. Top with the remaining layer. • Brush with the remaining syrup. • Heat the raspberry preserves in a saucepan until liquid. Spread over the cake. • Decorate with the extra raspberries. • Refrigerate for 1 hour.

1 Basic Sponge Cake (see page 30)

1 lb (500 g) fresh raspberries
  + about 15 extra, to decorate
1²/₃ cups confectioners' (icing) sugar
1 cup (250 ml) kirsch
1 package (8 oz/250 g) cream cheese,
  softened
1 tablespoon finely grated lemon zest
2 tablespoons unflavored gelatin
¹/₄ cup (60 ml) cold water
1¹/₄ cups (300 ml) heavy (double)
  cream
1 cup (300 g) raspberry preserves
  (jam), strained, to remove the seeds

Cream Sponge
with passion fruit frosting

Basic Sponge: Preheat the oven to 375°F (190°C/gas 5). • Butter two 9-inch (23-cm) round cake pans. Line with parchment paper. • Mix the cornstarch, flour, baking powder, and salt in a small bowl. • Beat the egg yolks and sugar in a large bowl with an electric mixer at high speed until pale and thick. • Use a large rubber spatula to fold in the dry ingredients. • With mixer at high speed, beat the egg whites in a large bowl until stiff peaks form. Fold them into the batter. • Spoon half the batter into each of the prepared pans. • Bake for about 20 minutes, or until a toothpick inserted into the center comes out clean. • Cool the cakes in the pans for 5 minutes. Turn out onto racks. Carefully remove the paper and let cool completely. • Cream Filling: Beat the cream, vanilla, and sugar in a medium bowl with mixer on high speed until stiff. Frosting: Beat the confectioners' sugar, passion fruit pulp, and butter in a medium bowl. • Place one cake on a serving plate. Spread with the cream. Top with the remaining cake. Spread with the frosting.

Basic Sponge
1 cup (150 g) cornstarch (cornflour)
2 tablespoons all-purpose (plain) flour
1/2 teaspoon baking powder
1/4 teaspoon salt
4 large eggs, separated
1 cup (200 g) sugar

Cream Filling
1 cup (250 ml) heavy (double) cream
1/2 teaspoon vanilla extract (essence)
2 tablespoons sugar

Frosting
2 cups (300 g) confectioners' (icing) sugar
7–8 tablespoons passion fruit pulp
1 tablespoon butter, melted

30

SERVES 6–8

PREPARATION 25 min

COOKING 30 min

DIFFICULTY level 2

Chocolate Sponge
with cream filling

Preheat the oven to 375°F (190°C/gas 5). • Butter two 8-inch (20-cm) round cake pans. Line with parchment paper. • Mix the flour, cocoa, baking powder, and salt in a medium bowl. • Beat the egg yolks and sugar in a large bowl with an electric mixer at high speed until pale and thick. • With mixer at low speed, gradually beat in the dry ingredients, alternating with the milk. • With mixer at high speed, beat the egg whites in a large bowl until stiff peaks form. Fold them into the batter. • Spoon half the batter into each of the prepared pans. • Bake for about 30 minutes, or until springy to the touch and the cake shrinks from the pan sides. • Cool the cakes in the pans for 5 minutes. Turn out onto racks. Carefully remove the paper and let cool completely. • Place one cake on a serving plate and spread with the filling. Top with the remaining cake. Spread the top with the frosting.

1 cup (150 g) all-purpose (plain) flour
4 tablespoons unsweetened cocoa powder
1 teaspoon baking powder
1/4 teaspoon salt
4 large eggs, separated
1 cup (200 g) sugar
1/4 cup (60 ml) milk
1 quantity Cream Filling (see page 30)
1 quantity Chocolate Rum Frosting (see page 22)

SERVES 6–8

PREPARATION 30 min

COOKING 15-20 min

DIFFICULTY level 3

Almond Roll

with caramel crunch

Preheat the oven to 350°F (180°C/gas 4). • Butter a 10½ x 15½-inch (25 x 35-cm) jelly-roll pan. Line with parchment paper. • Caramel Crunch: Oil a baking sheet. Cook the sugar and almonds in a saucepan over low heat, stirring constantly, until the sugar melts. Simmer, stirring frequently, until deep golden brown. • Pour onto the prepared sheet and set aside to cool. • Crush into small pieces. • Roll: Beat the egg yolks and sugar in a large bowl with an electric mixer at high speed until pale and thick. • Add the almonds and almond extract. • With mixer at high speed, beat the egg whites and salt in a large bowl until stiff peaks form. • Fold them into the almond mixture. • Spoon the batter into the prepared pan. • Bake for 15–20 minutes, or until a toothpick inserted into the center comes out clean. • Turn the cake out onto a clean kitchen towel dusted with the confectioners' sugar. Carefully roll the cake up. • Beat the cream in a bowl until stiff. • Unroll the cake and spread with the cream. Reroll the cake. • Press the caramel pieces into the roll.

Caramel Crunch
1½ cups (300 g) sugar
¾ cup (100 g) blanched whole almonds

Roll
5 large eggs, separated
¾ cup (150 g) sugar
⅓ cup (50 g) finely ground almonds
1 teaspoon almond extract (essence)
¼ teaspoon salt
3 tablespoons confectioners' (icing) sugar, to dust

1½ cups (375 ml) heavy (double) cream

Lemon Roll
with almonds

Preheat the oven to 400°F (200°C/gas 6). • Butter a 15½ x 10½-inch (25 x 35-cm) jelly-roll pan. Line with parchment paper. • Beat the eggs, sugar, and salt in a medium bowl with an electric mixer at high speed until pale and thick. • Fold in the flour. • Spoon the batter into the prepared pan. • Bake for 8–10 minutes, or until springy to the touch. • Turn the cake out onto a clean kitchen towel dusted with the confectioners' sugar. Carefully roll the cake up. • Lemon Cream: Beat the egg and egg yolks, ½ cup (100 g) sugar, and lemon juice in a double boiler. Cook over low heat, stirring constantly with a wooden spoon, until the mixture lightly coats a metal spoon or registers 160°F (71°C) on an instant-read thermometer. Add the butter. Plunge the pan into a bowl of ice water and stir until cooled. • Syrup: Cook the lemon zest, sugar, and ¼ cup (60 ml) water in a saucepan over medium heat. Cook for 3–4 minutes, until the water is slightly reduced. • Strain, discarding the zest. Stir the remaining water and the rum into the syrup. • Unroll the cake and brush with the syrup. Spread the cake evenly with the lemon cream. • Reroll the cake and refrigerate for 2 hours. • Warm the apricot preserves and spread over the roll. Sprinkle with the almonds.

2 large eggs
⅓ cup (75 g) sugar
¼ teaspoon salt
⅔ cup (100 g) all-purpose (plain) flour
2 tablespoons confectioners' (icing) sugar
½ cup (150 ml) apricot preserves (jam)
1 cup (125 g) slivered almonds

Lemon Cream
1 large egg + 5 large egg yolks
¾ cup (350 g) sugar
2 tablespoons freshly squeezed lemon juice
¼ cup (60 g) butter, melted

Syrup
Zest of 1 lemon, cut into thin strips
¼ cup (50 g) sugar
½ cup (125 ml) water
¼ cup (60 ml) rum

SERVES 6–8

PREPARATION 30 min + 2 h to chill

COOKING 15 min

DIFFICULTY level 3

Sponge Roll
with chocolate hazelnut cream

Preheat the oven to 350°F (180°C/gas 4). • Line a 10 x 15-inch (25 x 35-cm) jelly-roll pan with parchment paper. • Beat the egg yolks, confectioners' sugar, and vanilla in a large bowl until pale and creamy. • Fold in the flour and cornstarch. • Beat the egg whites and salt with an electric mixer at high speed until stiff. Gently fold them into the batter. • Spoon the batter into the prepared pan. • Bake for about 15 minutes, or until risen and golden. • Dust a clean kitchen towel with confectioners' sugar. Turn the cake out onto the towel. Roll up the cake, using the towel as a guide. Leave, seam side down, until cool. • Unroll the sponge. Drizzle with the rum and cover with the chocolate spread. Roll up using the towel as a guide. Wrap the roll in foil. Chill for 2 hours. • Unwrap and transfer to a serving dish. • Dust with confectioners' sugar and sprinkle with the chocolate.

1 cup (150 g) confectioners' (icing) sugar + extra, to dust
4 large eggs, separated
1/3 cup (50 g) all-purpose (plain) flour
1 teaspoon vanilla extract (essence)
2 tablespoons cornstarch (cornflour)
1/4 teaspoon salt
3 tablespoons rum
1/2 cup (125 g) chocolate hazelnut spread (Nutella), softened
4 tablespoons grated dark chocolate

Sponge Roll
with raspberry cream

Preheat the oven to 400°F (200°C/gas 6). • Butter and flour a 10 x 15-inch (25 x 35-cm) jelly-roll pan. Line with parchment paper. • Mix the flour, baking powder, and salt in a medium bowl. • Beat the egg yolks, sugar, and vanilla in a large bowl with an electric mixer at high speed until pale and thick. • With mixer at low speed, gradually beat in the dry ingredients, alternating with the milk. • With mixer at high speed, beat the egg whites and cream of tartar in a large bowl until stiff peaks form. • Gently fold them into the batter. • Spoon the batter into the prepared pan. • Bake for about 15 minutes, or until lightly browned. • Dust a clean kitchen towel with confectioners' sugar. Turn the cake out onto the towel. Roll up the cake, using the towel as a guide. Leave, seam side down, until cool. • Filling: Process the raspberries until smooth. Strain out the seeds. • Beat the cream and sugar in a large bowl until stiff. Fold in the raspberries and pistachios. • Unroll the cake and spread with the filling. Reroll the cake. Place on a serving dish and dust with the confectioners' sugar.

1 cup (150 g) all-purpose (plain) flour
1½ teaspoons baking powder
¼ teaspoon salt
3 large eggs, separated
1 cup (200 g) sugar
1 teaspoon vanilla extract (essence)
¼ cup (60 ml) milk
¼ teaspoon cream of tartar

Filling
1 cup (150 g) fresh raspberries
1½ cups (375 ml) heavy (double) cream
¼ cup (50 g) sugar
¼ cup (25 g) pistachios, coarsely chopped
4 tablespoons confectioners' (icing) sugar, to dust

SERVES 6–8

PREPARATION 30 min

COOKING 15 min

DIFFICULTY level 2

Coffee Roll

Preheat the oven to 400°F (200°C/gas 6). • Butter a 10 x 15-inch (25 x 35-cm) jelly-roll pan. Line with parchment paper. • Mix the flour, baking powder, and salt in a large bowl. • Beat the eggs and 1 cup (200 g) of sugar in a large bowl with an electric mixer at high speed until pale and thick. • With mixer at low speed, gradually beat in the dry ingredients, alternating with the butter and coffee mixture. • Spoon the batter into the prepared pan. • Bake for about 20 minutes, or until springy to the touch. • Dust a clean kitchen towel with confectioners' sugar. Turn the cake out onto the towel. Roll up the cake, using the towel as a guide. Leave, seam side down, until cool. • Unroll the cake and spread evenly with the coffee-flavored cream filling. Reroll the cake.

1 cup (150 g) all-purpose (plain) flour
1 teaspoon baking powder
1/4 teaspoon salt
5 large eggs
1 cup (200 g) + 2 tablespoons sugar
1/3 cup (90 g) butter, melted
2 tablespoons freeze-dried coffee granules dissolved in 1 tablespoon boiling water
1 quantity Cream Filling (see page 30), flavored with 2 tablespoons freeze-dried coffee granules

Sénateur

Preheat the oven to 450°F (250°C/gas 8). • Line 3 baking sheets with parchment paper. • Unroll the pastry and cut into three 10-inch (25-cm) rounds. Prick with a fork. Place on the baking sheets. • Bake for 10–15 minutes, or until golden brown. • Cool on racks. • Vanilla Pastry Cream: Beat the egg yolks and sugar until pale and thick. Beat in the flour. Bring the milk to a boil with the salt and vanilla, then stir into the egg and sugar. Simmer over low heat, stirring constantly, until the mixture lightly coats a metal spoon or registers 160°F (71°C) on an instant-read thermometer. Stir the kirsch into the pastry cream and let cool. • Place one pastry round on a serving plate and spread with half the pastry cream. Cover with another layer of pastry cream and top with the remaining pastry round. • Heat the jelly in a small saucepan over low heat. Spread over the top and sides of the cake. Press the almonds into the sides and sprinkle over the top. Decorate with the fruit.

1½ lb (750 g) frozen puff pastry, thawed
1 tablespoon kirsch or other fruit liqueur
1 cup (300 g) red currant jelly
1 cup (125 g) toasted flaked almonds
Fresh red currants (or other berry fruit), to decorate

Vanilla Pastry Cream
5 large egg yolks
¾ cup (150 g) sugar
⅓ cup (50 g) all-purpose flour
2 cups (500 ml) whole milk
Pinch of salt
½ teaspoon vanilla extract (essence)

Mousse Cake

Mousse: Melt the white chocolate in a double boiler over barely simmering water. Set aside to cool. • Beat the cream cheese and sugar in a large bowl with an electric mixer at medium speed until smooth. • Add the white chocolate. • Sprinkle the gelatin over the orange juice in a saucepan. Let stand 1 minute. Stir over low heat until the gelatin has completely dissolved. Set aside to cool for 30 minutes. • Beat the cooled orange juice into the cream cheese mixture. • With mixer at high speed, beat the cream in a medium bowl until stiff. • Use a rubber spatula to fold the cream into the cream cheese mixture. • Trim the rounded top off the cake. • Place the cake in a 10-inch (25-cm) springform pan. Pour the mousse over the cake and refrigerate for 6 hours. • Lemon Topping: Stir the lemon juice and sugar in a saucepan over low heat until the sugar has dissolved. Remove from the heat and stir in the gelatin until dissolved. Set aside to cool. • Pour the topping over the mousse and refrigerate for 6 hours, or until set. • Loosen and remove the pan sides. Decorate with the kiwi.

Mousse

6 oz (180 g) white chocolate, coarsely chopped

2 packages (3 oz/90 g each) cream cheese, softened

1/4 cup (50 g) sugar

4 teaspoons unflavored gelatin

1/3 cup (90 ml) freshly squeezed orange juice

1 1/2 cups (375 ml) heavy (double) cream

1 Butter Cake (see page 12)

Lemon Topping

1/2 cup (125 ml) freshly squeezed lemon juice

1/4 cup (50 g) sugar

1 teaspoon unflavored gelatin

3–4 medium kiwifruit, peeled and sliced

SERVES 6–8

PREPARATION 20 min

COOKING 20 min

DIFFICULTY level 1

Fruity Heart

Preheat the oven to 400°F (200°C/gas 6.) • Butter and flour a 9-inch (23-cm) heart-shaped pan. • Unfold or unroll the pastry on a lightly floured surface into a 13-inch (33-cm) round. Fit the pastry into the prepared pan. Fold over and crimp the edges. Prick all over with a fork. • Line the pastry shell with foil and fill with dried beans or pie weights. Bake for 10 minutes, then remove the foil with the beans. Bake until crisp and golden brown. • Cool on a rack for 10 minutes. Carefully remove from the pan and let cool completely. • Arrange the strawberries on the cooled pastry, rounded side up. • Warm the red currant jelly and kirsch in a small saucepan. Brush over the strawberries. • Beat the cream and sugar in a medium bowl until stiff. Pipe rosettes over the cake.

8 oz (250 g) frozen puff pastry, thawed

1½ lb (750 g) fresh strawberries (preferably all about the same size), hulled and cut in half

1 cup (300 g) red currant jelly

2 tablespoons kirsch or other fruit liqueur

½ cup (125 ml) heavy (double) cream

1 tablespoon sugar

SERVES 8–10

PREPARATION 1 h + 1 h to chill + time to prepare cake

COOKING 15 min

DIFFICULTY level 3

Coffee Heart

Prepare the cake. • Truffles: Melt the chocolate with the cream in a double boiler over barely simmering water. Set aside to cool. • Dissolve the coffee in the liqueur and stir into the chocolate mixture. Refrigerate for 1 hour, or until thick and malleable. • Roll teaspoonfuls of the chocolate mixture into round truffles and place on a dish lined with parchment paper. This should yield about 12 truffles. Cover and refrigerate until firm. • Coffee Buttercream: Melt the white chocolate with the cream in a double boiler over barely simmering water. Set aside to cool. • Beat the butter in a large bowl with an electric mixer at high speed until creamy. Gradually beat in the confectioners' sugar. • Beat in the chocolate mixture and dissolved coffee. • Split the cake horizontally. Place one layer on a serving plate and spread with a quarter of the buttercream. Place the remaining layer on top. Spread with the buttercream. • Press the hazelnuts into the sides of the cake. Arrange the truffles on top. Dust with cocoa.

1 Butter Cake (see page 12), baked in a 9-inch (23-cm) heart-shaped cake pan

Truffles

4 oz (125 g) dark chocolate, chopped

3 tablespoons heavy (double) cream

2 teaspoons freeze-dried coffee granules

1/2 tablespoon coffee liqueur

Coffee Buttercream

10 oz (300 g) white chocolate, chopped

2/3 cup (180 ml) heavy (double) cream

1 3/4 cups (450 g) butter, softened

1 cup (150 g) confectioners' (icing) sugar

1 tablespoon freeze-dried coffee granules dissolved in 1 tablespoon boiling water, cooled

1 cup (100 g) hazelnuts, toasted and coarsely chopped

1/4 cup (30 g) unsweetened cocoa powder, to dust

Simnel Cake

Preheat the oven to 325°F (170°C/gas 3). • Butter a 9-inch (23-cm) springform pan. Line with parchment paper. Butter the paper. • Mix the flour, nutmeg, allspice, baking powder, baking soda, and salt in a large bowl. • Beat the butter and sugar in a large bowl with an electric mixer at medium speed until creamy. • Add the eggs, one at a time, beating until just blended after each addition. • With mixer on low, gradually beat in the dried fruit, 3 tablespoons of sherry, both zests, and the dry ingredients. • Roll out half the marzipan on a board dusted with confectioners' sugar to a 9-inch (23-cm) round. Spoon half the batter into the prepared pan. Place the marzipan on top. Spoon in the remaining batter. • Bake for 2 hours, or until a toothpick inserted into the center comes out clean. • Cool the cake in the pan for 1 hour. Loosen and remove the pan sides. Invert onto a rack. Loosen and remove the pan bottom. • Turn top-side up and let cool completely. • Roll out the remaining marzipan to a 9-inch (23-cm) round. Trim around the marzipan with a fluted pastry cutter to make a decorative edge. Brush the cake with the remaining sherry and cover with the marzipan. Use a fork to make patterns on the top.

2 cups (300 g) all-purpose (plain) flour
1 teaspoon ground nutmeg
1 teaspoon ground allspice
1 teaspoon baking powder
1/2 teaspoon baking soda (bicarbonate of soda)
1/4 teaspoon salt
3/4 cup (180 g) butter, softened
1 cup (200 g) sugar
4 large eggs
3 cups (300 g) chopped mixed dried fruit
1/4 cup (60 ml) dry sherry
2 tablespoons finely grated orange zest
2 tablespoons finely grated lemon zest
1 lb (500 g) marzipan, softened
Ribbons, sugar eggs, and marzipan animals to decorate

SERVES 8–10

PREPARATION 50 min

COOKING 20 min

DIFFICULTY level 2

Chocolate Cake
with ricotta filling

Preheat the oven to 375°F (190°C/gas 5). • Butter two 9-inch (23-cm) round cake pans. • Stir the almonds, flour, cocoa, baking powder, and salt in a large bowl. • Beat the egg yolks, 1 cup (200 g) of sugar, and both extracts in a large bowl until pale and thick. • Gradually beat in the dry ingredients, alternating with the milk. • Beat the egg whites and remaining sugar in a large bowl until stiff, glossy peaks form. Fold into the batter. • Spoon half the batter into each of the prepared pans. • Bake for about 20 minutes, or until a toothpick inserted into the center comes out clean. • Cool in the pans for 10 minutes. Turn out onto racks and let cool completely. • Ricotta Filling: Beat the cream in a medium bowl until stiff. • Beat the ricotta, confectioners' sugar, and candied peel in a food processor until smooth. Fold the cream into the ricotta mixture. • Split the cakes horizontally. Place one layer on a serving plate. Spread with one-third of the filling. Repeat with two more layers. Place the remaining layer on top. Spread with the frosting. Decorate with the shavings.

1½ cups (225 g) finely ground almonds
⅔ cup (100 g) cake flour
⅔ cup (100 g) unsweetened cocoa powder
1½ teaspoons baking powder
¼ teaspoon salt
8 large eggs, separated
1½ cups (300 g) sugar
2 teaspoons vanilla extract (essence)
½ teaspoon almond extract (essence)
½ cup (125 ml) milk

Ricotta Filling
1 cup (250 ml) heavy (double) cream
2 cups (500 g) ricotta, drained
½ cup (75 g) confectioners' (icing) sugar
½ cup (50 g) chopped peel
1 quantity Chocolate Frosting (see page 24)
Shavings of dark chocolate, to decorate

SERVES 10–12
PREPARATION 30 min + time to
prepare sponge
COOKING 25 min
DIFFICULTY level 2

Party Cake

Prepare the sponge. • Cake: Preheat the oven to 325°F (170°C/gas 3). • Set out a baking sheet. • Bring the milk, coffee beans, and lemon zest to a boil in a saucepan over medium heat. • Remove from the heat and add the vanilla. • Beat the egg yolks and sugar in a large bowl with an electric mixer at high speed until pale and thick. • Use a large rubber spatula to fold in the flour. • Gradually add the milk mixture. Return the mixture to the saucepan and cook over low heat, stirring constantly with a wooden spoon, until the mixture lightly coats a metal spoon or registers 160°F (71°C) on an instant-read thermometer. Discard the coffee beans and lemon zest. • Split the cake horizontally. Drizzle with the amaretto. • Place one layer on the baking sheet. Spread with the filling. Top with the remaining layer. • Topping: With mixer at high speed, beat the egg whites in a large bowl until stiff peaks form. Add the liqueur. • Spread the top of the cake with the frosting. Bake for about 25 minutes, or until lightly browned. • Decorate with the marzipan flowers.

1 Basic Sponge Cake (see page 30)

Filling
2 cups (500 ml) milk
3 coffee beans
Zest of 1 lemon, in one piece
1 teaspoon vanilla extract (essence)
4 large egg yolks
1 cup (200 g) sugar
1/3 cup (50 g) all-purpose (plain) flour
2 tablespoons amaretto (almond liqueur)

Topping
2 large egg whites
2 tablespoons confectioners' (icing) sugar
1 teaspoon Alchermes liqueur or marsala wine
Marzipan flowers, to decorate

Florentine Cake

Preheat the oven to 350°F (180°C/gas 4). • Butter and flour an 8-inch (20-cm) pan. • Mix the flour, baking powder, and salt in a bowl. • Beat the eggs, sugar, and vanilla in a large bowl with an electric mixer at high speed until pale and creamy. • Fold in the dry ingredients. • Spoon the batter into the prepared pan. • Bake for 40–45 minutes, or until a toothpick inserted into the center comes out clean. • Turn out onto a rack to cool. • Filling: Mash the raspberries, sugar, and liqueur in a bowl. • Beat the cream until stiff. Fold into the raspberry mixture. • Cut the cake in $\frac{1}{2}$-inch (1-cm) slices. • Line a 6-cup (1.5-liter) pudding mold with cake. Spread with one-third of the raspberry mixture. Top with a layer of cake and spread with a third of the raspberry mixture. Repeat and top with a layer of cake. Cover with plastic wrap (cling film) and chill for 3 hours. • Topping: Beat the egg whites and sugar in a large bowl until stiff peaks form. • Turn the cake out onto a platter. Spread with the meringue. • Broil (grill) 6–8 inches from the heat source until lightly browned. Decorate with the raspberries and almonds.

1 cup (150 g) all-purpose (plain) flour
1 teaspoon baking powder
$\frac{1}{4}$ teaspoon salt
4 large eggs
$\frac{3}{4}$ cup (150 g) sugar
$\frac{1}{2}$ teaspoon vanilla extract (essence)

Filling
$1\frac{1}{2}$ cups (250 g) fresh raspberries
$\frac{3}{4}$ cup (150 g) sugar
2 tablespoons orange liqueur
$\frac{1}{2}$ cup (125 ml) heavy (double) cream

Topping
3 large egg whites
$\frac{3}{4}$ cup (150 g) sugar
Fresh raspberries, to decorate
Flaked almonds, to decorate

Meringue Cake

Cake: Preheat the oven to 325°F (160°C/gas 3). • Butter a 9-inch (23-cm) springform pan. Line with parchment paper. • Mix the flour and salt in a medium bowl. • Beat the eggs, egg yolks, and sugar in a large bowl with an electric mixer at high speed until pale and thick. • Fold in the dry ingredients. • Spoon the batter into the prepared pan. • Bake for 40–50 minutes, or until a toothpick inserted into the center comes out clean. • Cool the cake in the pan for 5 minutes. Invert onto a rack. Remove the paper and let cool. • Syrup: Bring the sugar and water to a boil in a saucepan over medium heat. Boil for 5 minutes, stirring constantly. Remove from the heat and stir in the walnuts and caramel flavoring. • Preheat the oven to 350°F (180°C/gas 4). • Slice the cake in three horizontally. Place one layer in the bottom of a pan or baking dish with tall sides and slightly larger than the cake. • Spoon one-third of the syrup over the cake. Repeat with the remaining 2 layers and the syrup. • Meringue: With an electric mixer at high speed, beat the egg whites, sugar, water, and cream of tartar until stiff, glossy peaks form. • Spread over the cake. • Bake for 8–10 minutes, or until lightly browned. • Cool the cake completely in the pan on a rack.

Cake
1¼ cups (180 g) all-purpose (plain) flour
¼ teaspoon salt
3 large eggs + 5 large egg yolks
¾ cup (150 g) sugar

Syrup
1½ cups (300 g) sugar
1 cup (250 ml) water
1 cup (125 g) walnuts, coarsely chopped
3 tablespoons caramel flavoring

Meringue
5 large egg whites,
¼ cup (50 g) sugar
5 teaspoons water
¼ teaspoon cream of tartar

SERVES 6–8

PREPARATION 30 min

COOKING 1 h 30 min

DIFFICULTY level 2

Meringue Cake
with candied chestnuts

Preheat the oven to 250°F (130°C/gas ½). • Cut four 8-inch (20-cm) rounds of parchment paper and place on two baking sheets. • Mix the sugar and confectioners' sugar in a medium bowl. • Beat the egg whites with half the sugar mixture and salt in a large bowl with an electric mixer at medium speed until stiff, glossy peaks form. Gradually beat in the remaining sugar mixture. • Spread a quarter of the meringue mixture on each parchment round. • Bake for about 1 hour 30 minutes, or until crisp and pale gold. • Turn the oven off and let cool with the door ajar. • Carefully remove the paper. • Beat the cream and vanilla in a large bowl until stiff. • Fold in the chocolate chips and candied chestnuts. • Place one meringue round on a serving plate. Spread with one-third of the cream. Top with another meringue round and spread with one-third of the cream. Top with the last round and spread with the remaining cream. • Crumble the remaining meringue over the cake.

1 cup (200 g) sugar
⅔ cup (100 g) confectioners' (icing) sugar
6 large egg whites
¼ teaspoon salt
2 cups (500 ml) heavy (double) cream
½ teaspoon vanilla extract (essence)
6 tablespoons dark chocolate chips
4 candied chestnuts (marrons glacé), crumbled or coarsely chopped

SERVES 8–10

PREPARATION 1 h + 1 h to freeze

DIFFICULTY level 2

Ice Cream Cake
with strawberries

Mix the wine and kirsch in a small bowl and drizzle a little on each cake slice. Use the slices to line a 2-quart (2-liter) straight-sided soufflé dish. • Spoon one-third of the ice cream over the cake. Top with one-third of the strawberries. Cover with cake slices. Repeat with the ice cream, strawberries, and cake slices until they have all been used, finishing with a layer of ice cream. • Freeze for 1 hour. • Soak the dish in hot water for 10 seconds. Turn out onto a serving dish, ice cream-side facing up. Decorate with the strawberries.

$\frac{1}{2}$ cup (125 ml) dry white wine
$\frac{1}{4}$ cup (60 ml) kirsch
1 Butter Cake (see page 12), cut into $\frac{1}{2}$-inch (1-cm) thick slices
1 quart (1 liter) vanilla ice cream, softened
1 lb (500 g) strawberries, hulled and halved (reserve 10 to decorate)

SERVES 8–10

PREPARATION 30 min + 7 h to chill

COOKING 50 min

DIFFICULTY level 1

Cheesecake

with vanilla-orange filling

Base: Butter a 9-inch (23-cm) springform pan. • Mix the crumbs, sugar, and butter in a medium bowl. Press into the bottom and partway up the sides of the pan. • Refrigerate for 1 hour. • Filling: Preheat the oven to 350°F (180°C/gas 4). • Beat the cream cheese, sugar, orange zest, and vanilla in a large bowl with an electric mixer at medium speed until smooth. • Add the eggs, one at a time, beating until just blended after each addition. • With mixer at low speed, add the sour cream. • Spoon the filling into the crust. • Bake for about 50 minutes, or until set. • Cool the cake in the pan on a rack. • Refrigerate for 6 hours. Loosen and remove the pan sides to serve.

Base

2 cups (300 g) graham cracker (or digestive biscuit) crumbs

½ cup (125 g) butter, melted

¼ cup (50 g) sugar

Filling

1½ lb (750 g) cream cheese

1½ cups (300 g) sugar

2 tablespoons finely grated orange zest

2 teaspoons vanilla extract (essence)

4 large eggs

2 cups (500 ml) sour cream

Cheesecake
New York style

Base: Preheat the oven to 350°F (180°C/gas 4). • Butter a 9-inch (23-cm) springform pan. • Mix the crumbs, butter, and sugar in a medium bowl. Press into the bottom of the prepared pan. • Bake for 8–10 minutes. Cool completely in the pan on a rack. • Filling: Beat the cream cheese, sugar, and flour in a large bowl with an electric mixer at medium speed until creamy. Add the eggs, one at a time, beating until just blended after each addition. Stir in the sour cream and vanilla. • Spoon the filling into the crust. • Bake for 50–60 minutes, or until set. Cool the cake in the pan on a rack. • Loosen and remove the pan sides. Refrigerate for 6 hours. • Serve with fresh fruit, if liked.

Base

2 cups (300 g) graham cracker (or digestive biscuit) crumbs

½ cup (125 g) butter, melted

¼ cup (50 g) sugar

Filling

1½ lb (750 g) cream cheese, softened

1 cup (200 g) sugar

3 tablespoons all-purpose (plain) flour

4 large eggs

1 cup (250 ml) sour cream

2 teaspoons vanilla extract (essence)

Fresh fruit, to serve (optional)

Cheesecake
with lime

Base: Set out a 9-inch (23-cm) springform pan. • Mix the crumbs, sugar, and butter in a medium bowl. Press into the bottom and partway up the sides of the pan. • Filling: Sprinkle the gelatin over the lime juice and water in a saucepan. Let stand 1 minute. • Beat the sugar, eggs, and lime zest into the lime juice. Cook over low heat, stirring constantly until the mixture lightly coats a metal spoon or registers 160°F (71°C) on an instant-read thermometer. Immediately plunge the pan into a bowl of ice water and stir until the egg mixture has cooled. • Beat the butter and cream cheese in a large bowl with an electric mixer at medium speed until creamy. • With mixer at low speed, add the lime mixture. • Refrigerate for 1 hour • With mixer at high speed, beat the cream in a large bowl until stiff. Use a large rubber spatula to fold the cream into the lime mixture. • Spoon the filling into the crust. Refrigerate for 3 hours before serving. Loosen and remove the pan sides to serve. Decorate with the lime slices.

Base
2 cups (300 g) graham cracker (or digestive biscuit) crumbs
$^1/_2$ cup (100 g) sugar
$^1/_2$ cup (125 g) butter, melted

Filling
2 tablespoons unflavored gelatin
1 cup (250 ml) freshly squeezed lime juice
$^1/_4$ cup (60 ml) water
$1^1/_2$ cups (300 g) sugar
5 large eggs
2 teaspoons freshly grated lime zest
$^1/_2$ cup (125 g) butter, softened
$1^1/_2$ lb (750 g) cream cheese, softened
$^1/_2$ cup (125 ml) heavy (double) cream
Fresh lime slices, to decorate

Italian Cheesecake

Base: Mix the flour, sugar, baking powder, and salt in a medium bowl. Add the butter, egg, and water until well blended. Press into a disk, wrap in plastic wrap (cling film), and refrigerate for 30 minutes. • Preheat the oven to 350°F (180°C/gas 4). • Butter and flour a 10-inch (25-cm) springform pan. • Roll the dough out on a lightly floured surface into a 10-inch (25-cm) round. Fit into the prepared pan, trimming the edges if needed. Prick with a fork. • Bake for 20–25 minutes, or until lightly browned. • Loosen and remove the pan sides. Cool completely on a rack. • Rice Filling: Bring the milk, lemon zest, and salt to a boil in a saucepan over medium heat. Stir in the rice and sugar and simmer for 25–30 minutes, or until the rice is tender, stirring occasionally. Remove from the heat. • Sprinkle the gelatin over the water in a saucepan. Let stand 1 minute. Stir over low heat until completely dissolved. Stir the gelatin into the rice mixture and refrigerate for 15 minutes. • Beat the cream in a large bowl with an electric mixer at high speed until stiff. • Stir the mascarpone, vanilla, and cream into the rice mixture. • Transfer the base to a serving plate. Place the springform pan sides around the crust. Spoon the filling into the prepared crust. Refrigerate for 1 hour, or until set. • Decorate with the berries. • Warm the preserves in a saucepan over low heat. Brush over the fruit. Refrigerate for 15 minutes. Loosen and remove the pan sides to serve.

Base
1 cup all-purpose (plain) flour
1/4 cup (50 g) sugar
1/2 teaspoon baking powder
1/4 teaspoon salt
1/4 cup (60 g) butter, melted
1 large egg
2 tablespoons water

Rice Filling
2 cups (500 ml) milk
2 tablespoons finely grated lemon zest
1/4 teaspoon salt
1 cup (200 g) short-grain rice
1/4 cup (50 g) sugar
1 tablespoon unflavored gelatin
1/4 cup (60 ml) cold water
1 cup (250 ml) heavy (double) cream
1 cup (250 g) mascarpone cheese
1 teaspoon vanilla extract (essence)

2 cups (300 g) mixed red berries
1/2 cup (100 g) apricot preserves (jam)

Index

Copyright © 2009 by McRae Books Srl

This English edition first published in 2009

All rights reserved. No part of this book may be reproduced in any form without the prior written permission of the publisher and copyright owner.

Cakes

was created and produced by McRae Books Srl

Via del Salviatino 1 – 50016 Fiesole, (Florence) Italy

info@mcraebooks.com

Publishers: Anne McRae and Marco Nardi

Project Director: Anne McRae

Design: Sara Mathews

Text: McRae Books archive

Editing: Carla Bardi

Photography: Studio Lanza (Lorenzo Borri, Cristina Canepari, Ke-ho Casati, Mauro Corsi, Gil Gallo, Leonardo Pasquinelli, Gianni Petronio, Stefano Pratesi, Sandra Preussinger)

Home Economist: Benedetto Rillo

Artbuying: McRae Books

Layouts: Aurora Granata, Filippo Delle Monache, Davide Gasparri

Repro: Fotolito Raf, Florence

ISBN 978-88-6098-080-9

Printed and bound in China